Wealthy Woman
wise choices

Mary Grate-Pyos
Personal Finance Writer

Wealthy Woman – Wise Choices
By Mary Grate-Pyos, Personal Finance Writer

Copyright © 2002 by Mary Grate-Pyos

Published by Financially Focused, Inc.
Burke, Virginia 22015
(703) 503-0795
www.financiallyfocused.com

All rights reserved. No part of this book may be reproduced or transmitted in any form or by any means, electronic or mechanical, including photocopying, recording or by any information storage and retrieval system without written permission from the author, except for the inclusion of brief quotations in a review.

ISBN 0-9722290-0-0

Book designed by Pamela Terry, Opus 1 Design
Edited by Rosalind Blunt
Photos by Wonderfile

Printed by United Graphics Inc.
Manufactured in the United States of America

Library of Congress Catalog Card Number: 2002093183

First Edition

This book is dedicated to my son, "Bree." You are destined for greatness. You are my heart, and I love you so much!

Larry, thanks so much for your love and patience. Mommy and Daddy, you are the greatest! I love you! Rosalind, you are a jewel! Thanks for your support! To Family and Friends, I thank for encouraging and challenging me to be my best. And most of all, to God who continues to abundantly bless me over and over and over again!

Wealthy Woman
wise choices

Mary Grate-Pyos
Personal Finance Writer

Financially Focused, Inc   ▲   Burke, Virginia

Table of Contents

Introduction		9
Chapter 1	Financial Affairs of Women	13
Chapter 2	Wise Choices for Wealthy Living	21
Chapter 3	Understanding the P.R.I.D.E. Concept	25
Chapter 4	Planning and Preparation	33
Chapter 5	Retirement Planning	41
Chapter 6	Investment Planning	45
Chapter 7	Debt Management	55
Chapter 8	Education and Excellence	69
Chapter 9	Psychology of Wealth	75
Chapter 10	Choose To Be Wise	81
Chapter 11	The Conclusion of the Matter	87

Introduction

I want to be the catalyst that empowers women. I want to be a catalyst that moves women toward financial freedom and out of confusion, complacency, and frustration. I want to be an example of a wealthy woman in my living, giving, loving, and especially in my finances. As I read the statistics about women, I am often burdened that so many women who I meet are the statistics that I read about. That troubles me because the road toward financial fitness consists of small steps that lead to wealth. Any woman can start her financial journey to wealth, and many know they should, but a large percentage choose to do nothing until faced with a financial crisis. The small steps to wealth building are not known, are ignored, or are covered in myths that never were truths for many women. I want to make a positive difference in the lives of women and share what has worked and continues to work for me financially. I will be the first to say that I do not know it all, but I do know that prosperity, abundance and wealthy living are goals that can be achieved by anyone. No, it is not all about money, but money does make a major difference in the lives of women to gain wealth and experience wealthy living. I want to make a difference, and it is my prayer that I will accomplish that by writing this book.

Many women may not have been taught about finances or may even believe in being provided for by another, more than likely their husband. I am not against any man who provides for his wife, but a woman needs to know about money management. It is nice to have someone care for you financially, but the notion of chivalry is no longer realistic. A divorce can leave a woman in a desperate financial situation and in a state of confusion about her finances. There is a saying, "God bless the child who has her own." I like to reword it and say, "God bless the woman who has her own." A wealthy woman has to know about money matters. She cannot leave that part of her life up to her husband, the government, her company, her parents, or any other source. She needs to know the hows, whys, whens, and how much about her personal finances. It is imperative that she knows. Divorce. Widowhood. Single marital status. Longer life span. All of these are reasons why a woman needs to know about money matters. Not only must she know about finances; she must take action. She must take the initiative and learn about basic money management. It is my hope that this book will be a step in the right direction that will move women to act now to provide for their own financial futures.

As you read this book, I hope that you are energized and motivated to move toward wealth and make the wise choices needed to reach your financial goals. If you are on track in reaching your goals, then share this book with another woman who needs to be empowered in her finances. Maybe it is your mother or sister. Maybe it is your daughter or niece. Help another woman on this journey of life to gain and experience financial freedom. The first step is acknowledgement. The next step is to act and do it now. Will you act now? Decide to make wise choices to become the wealthy woman you so richly deserve.

CHAPTER 1

Financial Affairs of Women

The statistics regarding women and retirement can be quite distressing. Women have, however, made great strides in achieving financial independence, but the need is still there to know and recognize the importance of taking control of their money matters. According to the Census Bureau, 75 percent of the elderly poor are female. Despite the strides women have made in closing the earning gap between men and women, the advancement in the workplace, and the increase in the number of women in educational institutions, women still remain unprepared for their financial futures. Women are living longer, but their retirement savings are not stretching to cover the additional years.

Reports say that the income for women overall is increasing, yet they are saving less for retirement. Women need to understand the importance of taking control of their financial future, and now is the appointed time to do so. Most women recognize this need, but often they postpone doing so. In the meantime, they fear what will happen and what the consequences will be for not being proactive and starting the process toward financial freedom. Frustration about money matters is a major motivator to get control of your financial future, but many women think that they lack the necessary skills and choose to do nothing. Make the wise choices and start today to take positive action steps that will move you from frustration to freedom in your money matters.

The more informed you become about the basics of managing money matters, the more empowered you are to act on wise choices to gain control over your money matters. Financial steps that you take today will greatly affect the life that you live tomorrow. Consider the financial consequences for not managing your money. You can experience high levels of debt, financial frustration, and insufficient retirement funds. Many women do not fare well in retirement. As a matter of fact, women make up a large percentage of the elderly poor. Women can positively affect their retirement and financial future. Women can change the lives of their mothers, their daughters, their nieces, and their sisters by educating themselves and others, sharing, and encouraging one another to save and invest. Will you accept this challenge?

Women are forced to take control of their finances during a crisis - illness, death of a spouse, divorce - not because they want to, but because they have to. So instead of having the appropriate mechanisms in place to meet financial challenges, many women are confronting financial issues during periods of emotional stress and strain. It is imperative to have a plan in place prior to being faced with some of life's challenges.

Women need to save and invest more than men because:

- Women live longer than men (thus needing a larger financial cushion to last longer through retirement);
- Women invest more conservatively than men (their financial portfolio earns less when they invest conservatively; thus they have to save more to make up the difference);
- Women leave their jobs more frequently than men (they are typically the primary caretaker of the home, thus less time in the work place to earn dollars for retirement);
- Women earn less than men (women earn approximately 73 percent of what men earn).

Time For Action

Women cannot afford to be ambivalent about money matters. Women need to take a more active role in being responsible for all aspects of their finances. Ponder these questions:

1. If my spouse came home today and said, "I am filing for a divorce," could I survive financially on my own?
2. If I lost my job/career today, could I survive financially if I am not gainfully employed for three months?

3. Am I listed in my spouse's will as his beneficiary or is the first wife still listed because someone forgot to make that minor change on the will?

4. Am I prepared financially for retirement?

5. Am I expecting Social Security to be my sole financial support during retirement?

6. Do I have sufficient savings and investments to sustain me in retirement?

It Is Your Responsibility

The fact is that the majority of women will be responsible for their own financial well-being as a result of getting a divorce or being widowed. Consider these daunting statistics:

- 95 % of all women will have sole responsibility for their finances, yet 79 % of all women have not planned for this.
- Women make up 85 % of occupants in nursing homes.
- 80 % of widows now living in poverty were not poor before the death of their husband.
- Divorce and widowhood may affect some 80-90 % of women during their lifetimes.
- The average asset value of a woman's retirement plan is $35,000.
- 75 % of the elderly poor are women. Approximately 7 out of 10 women will live in poverty.

- The median income of widowed and divorced women aged over 62 is under $10,000.

Some of the financial hindrances to women are based on myths and cultural rules that no longer benefit or empower them. You must make wise choices today that will positively affect your tomorrows. Let's explore a few of these myths:

Myth #1: My husband will take care of me.
Reality: Do not depend on your husband or significant other to provide for you financially. Yes, it is a wonderful option to have the love and support of a caring spouse who is willing to share his retirement earnings with you. However, with the current divorce rate, you really are taking a great risk assuming this to be true. God bless the woman who has her own and has planned for a solid financial future! Remember, you are responsible for your financial wellness. What someone else provides becomes extra savings and investment, but it is not a definite income that you should rely on.

Myth #2: Social Security will provide enough money for me to live comfortably during retirement.
Reality: This is so far from the truth. You need additional retirement dollars to supplement the funds that you receive from Social Security, and even that amount is questionable. The prongs of retirement planning include Social Security, pension, and personal savings and investments. An additional prong of retirement today is long-term care. We are living longer, and the need for long-term care is becoming a neces-

sity. The bottom line is that Social Security does not provide enough financial security for retirement. Start accumulating the necessary funds for your retirement. By saving small amounts on a regular basis, you can grow a very substantial nest egg that will complement your pension or employer sponsored retirement package.

Myth #3: I can't afford to save and invest.
Reality: The truth is that you cannot afford not to save and invest. Your comfort level in retirement will depend greatly on how well you prepare now. It does not require a large amount of money to invest. If you review carefully how and where you spend your money, I am sure that you can find enough money - at least $25 to $50 monthly - that you can use to start investing. It may not seem like a lot of money, but with time and the power of compounding, you can accumulate a nice financial cushion.

Myth #4: I don't need to know about money.
Reality: Women are being forced to handle their own finances, whether they want to or not. Make a concerted effort to become knowledgeable about money, investments and **YOUR** retirement. You cannot afford to be financially illiterate. The more you know about money matters, the wiser your choices, which results in better decisions regarding your financial security.

There Is Hope!

Here is the good news: **Now** is the appointed time to learn money management skills, regardless of your age or financial status! You are capable of planning, saving, and investing for your financial future. It will take discipline and a financial plan to get you to a wealthy place. Can you do it? Absolutely! Yes, you can!

*"Show me someone content with mediocrity,
and I'll show you someone destined for failure."*
                                        Johnetta Cole

CHAPTER 2

Wise Choices for Wealthy Living

Your life is all about choices. Your choices can either help or hinder you in this journey called life, especially in the area of finances. A choice that you make today can either propel you into a life of abundance and prosperity or can devastate your wellness and financial foundation. Life is about making right choices. When addressing money matters, it is best to make wise choices that lead to wealth and financial freedom.

There are many definitions of wealthy living. I define wealthy living as having enough of all of the essentials in life: love, great health, loving friends and family, spirituality, and of course, money. Enough money is based on your definition of what is required for you. Wealth, merely from a financial perspective, has varied dollar amounts based on what you think is enough to make you happy, but the dollar amount is not the key. Being wealthy is a total package of daily love, good living, giving, laughter, joy, peace of mind, serenity, and money, combined with absolute contentment for life just where you are. Your views about your money matters and your definition of wealth are personal decisions. Regardless of how you define wealth, your finances must be in order to enjoy the peace of mind that you deserve and to eliminate the stressors that result from not having your finances in order.

Your money decisions are your choices. Why not make them wise choices? Choose wealthy living. We live in the wealthiest country in the world, yet many choose to struggle financially on a daily basis, year after year. It is a choice. You can choose to buy assets that depreciate in value, or you can buy stocks in a company that appreciate over time. It is your choice to either attract or detract those situations in your life that bring peace of mind. It is your choice, on a daily basis, minute by minute, to speak doubting words of poverty or powerful words of prosperity. You have the choice to build a solid foundation by making wise choices about your money matters, or you can chip away at your foundation by being burdened with debt. It is your choice, and only you can set the goals to take powerful steps that empower you financially. You have the choice to develop financial goals, or you can choose to languish in procrastination as life's valuable time passes on.

The choices that we make in life are limited by our knowledge of what the options are that we can choose from to make a financial impact in our finances. Sometimes women are not exposed to all of the options, and neither do they take the time to explore the choices that are available to them. When it relates to money matters, what women do not know can and will hurt their financial future. Many women know what to do, but choose to do nothing. Make the wise choice today to get proactive about your money matters. You cannot afford to stand still as time passes and not become proactive in your money matters. Procrastination is also a choice, but it is always a painful price regardless of the situation. Become active about your money matters so that you can move in the direction of living abundantly, peaceably, and with assurance about your financial future.

As you read this book, I hope that you will discover ideas and strategies that you can use that will empower you to make wise choices. I want you to be enlightened and inspired to take action to move to a place of wealthy living that works for you. I hope that you will take action steps that will result in joy and peace in your daily moments. It is my vision that you will move from frustration to financial freedom as you continue this journey called life. Wealthy living is yours. You have the power to create your own financial destiny! Take the initiative and begin now. Choose today as the first day of your financial wellness.

CHAPTER 3

Understanding the P.R.I.D.E. Concept

If you take pride in something, you will make sure it looks its best, that it is taken care of, properly maintained, and protected from all harm or danger. This notion is how I feel women should be about their financial future. Every woman should manage her money with pride. She needs to make sure that her financial future is optimistic and secure. She also needs to make sure that she has the proper protection for the risks in her life by having sufficient life, health, and home insurance, as well as long term care and disability coverage. Managing your money with P.R.I.D.E. is my concept for this book. If a woman takes pride in her financial future, there are few money obstacles that she cannot handle.

It is imperative that women be involved in their own financial affairs. Many women will be solely responsible for managing their own finances as a result of being divorced or widowed. Women must participate in and become a major player in their financial lives. The P.R.I.D.E. concept I have devised teaches women how to manage their money matters by focusing on these 5 areas of money management:

P - Planning and Preparation

R - Retirement

I - Investment

D - Debt Management

E - Education and Excellence

Effectively managing your money and not letting your money manage you instills pride, boosts confidence and produces financial stability. Each of the components above is essential for novice investors who are just beginning the financial journey and also for seasoned savers and investors. Financial stability begins as a journey toward abundance, prosperity and wealthy living. Women are all at different stages of the financial journey, and they must continue to make wise choices if they want the freedom they deserve.

Planning and Preparation. Planning and preparation are the first steps in managing your money with pride. As you plan and prepare, it is essential that you develop a financial mission statement for your life. A financial mission statement sets the stage by establishing an overview of what you want to accomplish with your money. You put your financial mission statement in action by setting short and long term financial goals. Never underestimate the power of established financial goals.

Write your goals and keep them constantly before you as a reminder. Make your financial mission statement clear and follow the action steps to reach your short and long term goals. Financial success comes when you move toward your financial goals, thus rejecting every action that hinders your financial freedom. Charge card and other debts distract you from obtaining the financial freedom you deserve. Late fees and high interest rates minimize the amount that you have to save and invest. Take responsibility for your financial life by planning and preparing for every phase of your life. Take control of your own financial life as if your life is a business venture that you are managing. And yes, you are in the business of managing your financial life. Your financial life matters, so start planning and preparing now. You are worth the time and effort that you invest in yourself.

What are your reasons for working? Having a motive of financial preservation is an encouragement to plan and prepare for your financial future. Working to just pay debts is not enough incentive for me. Women need to move from just earning a living to enjoying life, even as they diligently earn and plan for their financial fitness. Make a concerted effort to plan why and how you spend your money. Take all of the necessary steps to secure your financial future by setting a vision and purpose for your money. Money with no direction becomes wasted money that gets frittered away on nonsense. The first step to empowerment in your money matters is to plan and prepare properly for wise use of your money. This is the foundation to taking pride and ownership of your financial affairs. Start the process and begin the journey to financial freedom.

Retirement Planning. After you have planned and prepared for your financial future, you can now take the essential steps in some key focus areas. Retirement planning is one of those areas that deserve your attention. For some women, the issue of a secure financial future begins only when they are close to retirement age. For some women, retirement is some ancient act so far in the future that they cannot conceive it, yet they think daily of how they can redirect their lives – how to leave that current place of employment, return to college, or just take a break and travel to places they only dreamed about. Retirement planning requires taking a serious look at wise choices that are needed for wealthy living. Having your financial house in order will allow you to retire with ease. You need to determine what your financial goals are and start saving and investing with those goals in mind. Retirement planning is a wise choice that contributes to long-term security and stability.

Investment Planning. Investing is so important to managing your money with pride. You want to keep up with inflation, and investing in the stock market is an excellent option even in a bear market. You must start investing now. You need to seek employment with companies that have retirement packages that provide a base for your financial nest egg. You must start asking for the salaries that you deserve. Steady look for opportunities to increase your income and net worth, and understand that there is a significant difference between the two. It is not impressive that you earn a million dollars. In a lifetime, most individuals do earn a million dollars. What impresses me is what you have done financially through incremental steps to preserve a million dollars. Yes, anyone can earn a million dollars, but most have a net worth that is far below that. Wise investment choices are essential to living a wealthy life.

Debt Management. My Dad says, "The trouble with trouble is that it always starts off as fun." That is how debt operates. When you do not understand the dangers of improper use of credit, it is such a thrill to be in possession of a credit card that brings you power, so you think. Power in the form of a credit card is power you can live without. Actually, there is no power in a credit card. Sure, it will allow you to have temporary financial freedom today, but nothing permanent on tomorrow that will result in financial security. It is interesting to me that 'debt' and 'death' sound so much alike. Debt operates just like death when it is not managed properly. Debt will and can kill your spirit, but with proper discipline, you can relieve yourself from this millennium style of slavery. Debt in its purest form is bondage. Once you understand debt for what it truly is, you will want to free yourself from this bondage to a place of personal financial freedom. Let go of old ways of money management that no longer empower you. A positive spin to eliminating debt in your life is to focus on increasing your net worth. Work at decreasing the liabilities that you owe and increasing the assets that you own. Your net worth is dependent on you adding to the proper side of this equation. The only financial future that you have is the one that you create for yourself.

Education and Excellence. Financial education is so important, especially for women. Women need to learn and know about basic money management, investing, and retirement planning. Financial education for women is essential. Financial education assists them in bringing forth the excellence in their lives. You can choose to live your life in mediocrity or strive for excellence in all of your endeavors, especially in the area of money management. Wise management of your money brings about joy and leads to excellence in other areas of your life. Get empowered through financial education. Encourage yourself and others to get in shape financially. Be definite in your learning and watch financial empowerment and wealthy living become realities in your life.

"If you fail to plan, you plan to fail."

CHAPTER 4

Planning and Preparation

The first step in the P.R.I.D.E. concept of money management is to plan and prepare for the financial life that you want. Every woman needs a strategy to properly prepare for her financial future. Planning for your financial future and making the necessary preparation are essential steps for building wealth and peace of mind. You must develop goals and objectives that state specifically what you want out of life as it relates to your finances and overall well-being. Your plan for your money gives you a view of what you want to accomplish and how you will need to manage your finances to make your plan a reality. It is important to seek the advice of others, such as a financial planner, tax accountant, and an attorney who will help you to develop strategies to meet your goals. However, you must establish the foundation from which these individuals will help you build your financial house. The planning and preparation process begins with you. Finances affect all areas of your life, so it is imperative that you decide how, when and why you spend your money. Planning and preparation will encompass your goals, visions, and dreams. You need a plan for your money. You need to plan and prepare for financial stability, investment opportunities and retirement. You need to plan and prepare for financial challenges which are sure to come. Some actions like debt happen as a result of NOT having a plan. Remember, money without a plan is money madness, so develop a plan for your finances and follow through with the necessary action steps. A plan helps to focus your dreams and provides a clear picture of how your finances will get you there.

A financial mission statement encompasses the core of who you are and who you want to become as it relates to your finances. State in your financial mission statement why you trek off to work each day. Your financial mission statement guides you and serves as a reminder of how you will govern yourself financially. If making wise decisions regarding your money matters is what you want to do, then it takes a conscious effort on your behalf to make it happen. Money with no purpose, no vision, and no goal is sheer madness.

Steps to Planning Your Financial Future

- **Assess where you are financially**. Take a look at your cash inflow and outflow. What are your assets? What is your net worth? Do you know how much debt you have? Do you know who your creditors are? Knowing your money flow is an important step toward financial freedom. Looking at how you spend your money helps to identify wise choices to make to change your spending habits and highlights where you can save more to reduce waste in your finances.

- **After assessing where you are financially, set realistic short and long term financial goals.** Your short and long term goals are the specific action steps that you need to take that make your financial mission statement a reality. The financial mission statement sets the stage, and the short and long term goals bring your statement to life. Maybe you want to be debt-free. Maybe you want to start investing or pay your bills on time so that you will not incur late fees. One of your goals could be to establish a college fund for your children. Whatever your goals are, make sure that you write them down. Keep them before you at all times and update them as your life circumstances change. Look at your goals at least monthly. Decide to move closer to financial freedom by setting short and long term goals. Determine what the projects are in your life and align your finances to accomplish them.

- **Determine how much income you will need for your financial future.** A common rule of thumb suggests that you will need at least 70 to 80 percent of your current income to maintain your current lifestyle. Bear in mind that you may need less if you plan to drastically change your lifestyle or need more if you are burdened with an enormous amount of debt while in retirement. If you want to calculate this amount yourself, there are numerous calculators on the Internet. You can also consult a financial planner who can assist you in determining your financial needs and help you develop strategies to reach your goals.

- **Take the necessary steps to secure your financial future**. If a secure financial future means investing more, then begin the process now. If paying yourself more and less to creditors solidifies your financial stability, then do it. It does not matter if you develop your own strategy or seek the advice of a financial planner; stay the course to secure your financial well-being.

After you have made your plans, make the proper preparation to get your financial house in order. The following steps will guide you in getting your financial affairs in order:

- **Organize your financial papers**. Organize your financial documents and store them in a safe place. This includes copies of insurance policies; titles and inventory of assets owned; bank and brokerage statements; copies of wills and pensions; retirement statements; list of creditors, including addresses, payment due dates, amounts owed; and account numbers for checking, savings, and brokerage accounts. Put these documents in a secure place that is readily available for quick reference.

- **Prepare and update your will.** Most Americans (50 %) do not have a will. If you are not comfortable with your state of residency dictating how your assets will be distributed, I strongly suggest that you prepare a will, regardless of how little you think you own. Each state has its own intestate laws on how your assets will be distributed in case you die without a will. If you do not have a will, there are a few options. You can have an attorney to prepare one for you. You can buy a form will and fill in the blanks, or you can buy a computer generated will and prepare it. Have an attorney review your will, regardless of the method of preparation.

- **Make an assessment of your insurance policies** - life insurance; health; disability and long-term care. Assess if you have sufficient insurance to manage the risks in your life. Also check to ensure that your insurance policies have the correct beneficiaries listed. Review insurance needs as life situations change, such as marriage, divorce, or birth of a child.

- **Review your credit report or establish credit if you have no credit.** Your credit report is a mirror of your personal financial health. It addresses your ability and willingness to pay, speaks about your character, and tells how you handle business transactions. Request a copy of your credit report from the three major credit bureaus: Equifax (800-685-1111); Experian (888-397-3742); and TransUnion (800-916-8800). Review your report and dispute any erroneous information. If there are extenuating circumstances that may have caused your credit rating not to be in pristine shape, then include a statement in your credit report to explain your situation. If you do not have credit established in your name, take the necessary steps to do so. Many women realize after being divorced or widowed that they need some level of credit established in their name. Obtaining credit does not mean that you have to abuse it, so take the necessary steps to establish it now.

- **Establish a "peace of mind" fund.** This is commonly known as an emergency fund. I believe in the positive approach to money management, thus a "peace of mind" fund to meet the financial challenges that you may face. Determine if you have financial reserves in place to sustain you if you are faced with a financial challenge. Could you leave a job that renders you stressed and frustrated at the end of each day? Could you redirect your life and start that business that you always wanted to start? Can you imagine being debt free and paying yourself the money that you are paying to creditors?

PLANNING AND PREPARATION

"The wise woman saves for the future, but the foolish woman spends whatever she gets."
                                       Proverbs 21:20 (LB)

CHAPTER 5

Retirement Planning

Your fiscal wellness in retirement is a compilation of all of your financial actions prior to reaching retirement status. To enjoy a retirement that is free from financial cares and concerns requires wise management of all of your resources and covers every aspect of financial planning. Having a secure retirement is not an easy task and the process is not to be taken lightly. It will require you to have a plan, which should be included in your financial mission statement, and in your long-term goals. The life that you enjoy in retirement is based on an accumulation of all of your financial actions prior to redirecting your life activities, which is how I view retirement. Retirement planning is based on your wise management of debt throughout your entire life; your long term, systematic approach to investment; and a consistent effort to increase your net worth annually. It requires an assessment of how much you will need for your 'golden' years and a thorough look at the strategies to help you reach your retirement goals.

For many women, retirement is such a distant event in the future. Retirement planning is much more than selecting a home to settle in on a beach front property. It requires a tough look at your lifestyle and financial resources, and must address issues such as disability insurance and long-term care. These issues, however, need to be addressed prior to your retirement years. The earlier you start saving and investing, the more likely you are to amass the resources needed prior to retirement. Women are living longer, thus requiring more resources to cover the additional years. You do not want to outlive your money, so retirement planning requires a concerted effort. So how much do you need for a secure retirement and how do you start the process? There are four prongs to retirement: (1) Pension; (2) Social Security; (3) Taxable Savings; and (4) Tax-deferred Savings. You may need to seek the advice of a financial planner or a retirement specialist to assist you in a comprehensive look at all of your resources, your retirement goals, and the strategies to make your retirement goals a reality. A retirement calculator can also be helpful in determining an estimate of what resources are needed during retirement. The following are the major decisions that must be considered when preparing for retirement:

- Decide when you want to retire.

- Determine - in today's dollars - the annual income you desire during your retirement years.

- Determine the average return you expect to get on your investments before and after retirement.

- Determine the current value of your current investments. This includes your individual retirement accounts, pension plans, as well as taxable accounts.

- Obtain an estimate of your future Social Security benefits. Ensure that you have provided to the Social Security Administration any name changes (marriage, divorce) so that all of your benefits are credited to you.

- Obtain an estimate of what benefits your company will provide during retirement.

You can have it all in retirement, but it will require more than a haphazard approach to the resources needed during your retirement years. The decisions that you make today will have a huge impact on your life on a daily basis in retirement. Over time, your wise choices compound dramatically, but the mistakes that you make or the actions you do not take also compound. To create the financial independence that you want to enjoy, you must plan accordingly, ask pertinent questions, and develop financial scenarios that address your needs and fund your retirement goals. You will need the best mix of investments for the long haul, and a long-term approach of investing in stocks is your best choice for a secure financial future.

*"The plans of the diligent lead to profit,
as surely as haste leads to poverty."*
                              Proverbs 21:5   (NIV)

CHAPTER 6

Investment Planning

Investing is not a mystery. It does, however, depend on your basic working knowledge of investing and your tolerance for risk. If you choose to invest on your own or decide to have a broker or investment advisor manage your investments for you, a good foundation of basic investment terms is a must and a major step in creating wealth. If you are a beginner investor and cannot decide if you should invest in stocks or mutual funds, read on to get a basic understanding of both. Remember, the best kind of investor is an informed investor, so whatever you invest in, always complete your research first.

A **stock** is partial ownership or equity in a company. When you buy stock in a company, you become a shareholder. There are **two basic types of stocks: common** and **preferred**. If you are a shareholder of common stocks, you are entitled to vote in the election of company officials and are entitled to receive dividends on your shares, if the company pays dividends. If you are a shareholder of preferred stocks, usually you do not have voting rights, but you receive a fixed dividend and are paid before common stockholders. **Dividends** are distributions of a company's profit or earnings back to the company's shareholders. Many companies offer **dividend reinvestment plans**, which means that instead of sending you a check for the dividends earned, the dividends are used to purchase additional shares of the company's stock. This is a great way to increase your investment in the company over a period of time. You can purchase stocks through a broker, through dividend reinvestment plans or directly through the company, which is known as **direct stock purchase**. Dividend reinvestment plans, also called DRIPs, are managed by a transfer agent (usually a bank) for the company. DRIPs and direct stock purchases allow the individual investor to purchase shares directly from the company.

To learn about a particular stock, request a copy of the company's **annual report**; search the internet; call the company and ask any questions that you may have; and track the stock in the news. As always, remember to research the company *before* becoming a shareholder. If you decide to invest in a stock, make sure that you diversify. **Diversification** simply means 'not putting all of your eggs in one basket.' Diversification means to invest in stocks in different industries so that you can minimize your loses as the market fluctuates from one day to the next.

A **mutual fund** is a professionally-managed pool of investment money from investors with similar investment objectives. A mutual fund represents many different sizes and industries of individual stocks and is managed by a fund manager. Mutual funds offer diversification and professional management of your money. As an investor in a mutual fund, you are buying shares of the fund known as the **net asset value**. Before investing in a mutual fund, find out if it is a **load** or **no-load fund**. A load is a commission to compensate the broker or sales agent who assisted in the purchase of a mutual fund. Load funds charge a sales commission; no-load funds do not charge a sales commission. If you pay a sales commission when you purchase the mutual fund, this is known as a **front-end load fund**. A commission paid when you sell the mutual fund is known as a **back-end load fund**.

Mutual funds are ideal for the investor who: (1) has a small amount of money to invest and wants to pool money with other investors; (2) does not want to risk losing money by investing all of it in an individual stock; (3) wants instant diversification; and (4) wants professional management of investment dollars. The first step toward creating wealth through mutual funds is to request a copy of the fund's prospectus. I agree that reading a prospectus can be a challenging feat and quite a humbling process. You can, however, glean from the prospectus the top holdings in the mutual fund to determine if those individual stocks are companies that you would invest in or purchase individually.

If by chance reading the prospectus is really out of your reach, call the company's Investor Relations and ask questions that you may have regarding the fund, such as the portfolio manager's experience; top holdings of the fund; minimum investment amount; and expense fees. Be sure to request materials including an application to open an account. Many mutual funds have great websites, so visit the Internet to get some of your questions answered. There are thousands of mutual fund companies to choose from, so do not get overwhelmed. Choose a few funds that you are interested in, send for the prospectus and application, complete the research, make a decision, and start investing.

Investing is a wise choice for your financial future

We choose to spend our money in many ways, but the majority of our income is spent on day-to-day living expenses. But even if you choose to live a simple life, it is imperative that you engage in investment planning to secure your financial future. A small amount of funds set aside each year can make a major difference in your long-term financial well-being and mental health. In order to have a financial future that supports you and your life goals, you will need to make the hard decisions to either delay gratification or give up a 'luxury' that you think you must have today in order to have the wealth that you need tomorrow. If you want to start investing, that may mean that you have to make the wise choice of postponing a vacation. The choices must be made.

Two of the greatest assets for your investment planning are time and compound interest. It is never too late to start investing. One of the financial mistakes that women make is not investing. I have heard women say, "I can't afford to invest." I have even heard these words, "I don't have enough money to invest." You can afford to invest and do have enough to invest if investing is a choice that you make. First, you cannot afford not to invest. Secondly, it does not require a large amount of money to start investing. What you do need is a consistent amount of money invested on a regular basis. That amount can be as small as $25 a month. As you invest and reinvest the dividends, the power of compounding produces a multiplication of your initial investment.

Consider these wise investing choices that will get you started in creating wealth in your life:

- **Contribute the maximum to your company's retirement plan.** If your employer provides a retirement plan, commit to participating, even if retirement is 20, 30 or even 40 years from today, but remember to diversify. Make sure that your portfolio does not consist entirely of your company's stock. Some employers offer matching funds, which is "free money" to add to your retirement account. If you feel that you cannot contribute the full amount that is allowed, contribute as much as you can. Most of the money invested in a retirement account is tax-free, which will also reduce your tax basis.

- **Start or join an investment club.** The National Association of Investors Corporation (NAIC) (www.betterinvesting.org) is an organization committed to assisting individuals and investment club members to create wealth by investing in the stock market. Membership for the individual investor is $39 annually and includes a monthly magazine, ***Better Investing***, a magazine written by investors for investors and dedicated to providing premier investment education. To start an investment club, the initial club dues are $40, and club membership fee for each member is $14. NAIC provides the mechanism to invest in approximately 150 companies by initially purchasing only one share of the stock directly from the company. The cost to you is a mere $7 - $10 to set up the account. **Starting and Running a Profitable Investment Club** by Thomas E. O'Hara and Kenneth S. Janke, Sr. is also an excellent book with valuable information to get you started. Gather a few like-minded friends, colleagues, or family members who are committed to increasing their wealth and get started on the road to investing.

- **Invest directly in individual stocks.** Many companies, such as Wal-Mart and IBM, allow you to invest directly to purchase stocks. Inquire with those companies that you are interested in if they have a dividend reinvestment plan (DRIP) or a direct stock purchase plan. If you can invest directly, request information including annual reports and other material on the financial performance of the company. I suggest that you have a long-term approach to investing and that you invest in quality stocks that have a strong past performance and pay dividends. Bear in mind that past performance is not a guarantee of future performance. Past performance does provide a barometer of a company's performance during a period of time in respect to market conditions. I emphasize always completing your research prior to investing. However, if you are not comfortable with investing in individual stocks, stick with the professional management of stocks by investing in mutual funds. Determine a set amount and have that amount automatically drafted from your checking account. You can invest directly in some companies beginning with as little as $25 monthly. The goal is to invest regularly with a long-term approach.

- **Invest in mutual funds.** You can also invest directly in mutual funds. Invest regularly and systematically. Many companies will waive the minimum investment amount when you agree to monthly deductions from your bank account. Make sure that you request a prospectus; complete your research on the mutual fund company; decide on a specific fund; and begin the process for investing for long-term.

It is never too late to start investing for your financial future. As you progress toward reaching your investment goals, help another woman to secure her financial foundation too!

"The trouble with trouble is that it often starts off as fun."
                                            Willie Ben Grate

CHAPTER 7

Debt Management

Think about your financial life for a moment. If you were to lose your job, how would you pay your bills? If you lost your job, would your family experience a major crisis immediately, or are you sheltered with savings and investments from your financial burdens?

Plain and simple, being in debt is bondage. Most Americans are in debt, but there is no reason for you, a wealthy woman, to be like average Americans and continue this debt trend. Dare to be positively different in your money matters. Being in debt is a debilitating action that affects all areas of your life. Debt robs you of peace of mind that you so richly deserve. It is an awful partner. Debt robs you of joy, kills your peaceful spirit, and gets in the way of you being all that you need to be to live and walk in your purpose. Is now the time for you to make the decision to be debt-free? Getting in debt is an easy feat, but it requires focus, determination, and discipline to become debt-free. As a matter of fact, it is a lack of focus and financial discipline that causes debt. Consider correcting your financial ways today so that you will have something worth talking about on tomorrow. Get committed to planning your freedom from the bondage of debt. Having full access to all of your money is a powerful step to living a peaceful, joyful life.

Here is a thought to consider. Are you living the life that you intended to live or are you living a life based on false values? These false values are based on those with whom you have compared yourself or your idea of what you think you should have without any regard to whether you can afford it or not. Debt is based on false values. If you know that you cannot afford a purchase, then you choose to buy it based on the values of someone whom you may have compared yourself to or something with which you want to identify yourself.

Most wealthy women have little or no outstanding debt. You must be clear that if you are making a payment to a creditor, you are **NOT** the owner of the property. Unless you are the possessor of a title or a piece of paper stating you as the owner, you are not. Make a mental shift, and this will free you financially.

Explore Your Value System to Manage Debt

If you are in debt, I challenge you to take a look at your value system or the values of other people or things that you may have attached to your own life. Your value system determines the amount of money you spend, affects how you spend, and affects how often you spend. A woman who is content with who she is has spending habits and purchasing power that match her own value system. This value-based management of debt will make you question your purchases, even the car that you drive and the clothes that you wear.

Is the life you are living based on what you actually want or is it based on what you think you should have? Advertisements are a key factor in understanding the value-based concept in understanding your relationship with debt. Take a look at advertisements that use movie stars and individuals of prominence to endorse their products. This marketing ploy has one underlying theme: that you will attach yourself to that person's value system and do whatever, whether financially feasible or not, to get that product or to project that image. You are introduced to an item by someone you admire who endorses a product that now you "just have to have." In a nutshell, you have made the choice to purchase an item based on the values of another. The result is debt, debt, and more debt. I challenge you to stop the cycle. Recognize why you purchase and spend the way that you do, and start identifying your value system. People who are heavily in debt or have filed for bankruptcy will benefit a great deal in identifying why they have to spend. Is it to keep pace with the neighbors, not realizing that the neighbors next door are the millionaires you read about? Is your purchasing power associated with an image that you think you are *supposed* to have because of your educational level or position at your place of employment?

Your debt level can also be associated with the value that you place on your own life. I believe that the issues we silently harbor in our hearts are expressed very loudly in how we spend our money. Your issues could be emotional, spiritual, physical, or social, but they will be expressed financially. It appears that we try to compensate for our issues and challenges in life by our spending. A quick view of your cash outflow will highlight the inner thoughts and patterns of your heart and mind.

What motivates you financially?

Are you motivated by need or a constant greed? A wise choice to consider is to analyze your spending. I know it may be painful, but it is essential for financial stability and will help you to identify where you can cut spending and save more. What are the financial triggers that cause you to spend? Do you spend because you are sad? Do you shop to relieve an anxiety? When you get depressed, do you spend, spend, and spend? Do you find yourself paying your credit card balance in full and then start charging again the next month? Does watching television trigger your spending urges? Very seldom do I watch television, but when I do, I drive my family crazy because I mute the television during commercials. I refuse to be tempted by advertisements. I am fully aware of the mind games used to convince consumers to make impulsive purchases. It is a marketing strategy, and I choose not to be a part of the game.

Escape from Debt

Many times we move from what was a financial crunch and plunge deep into a financial crisis. Instead of analyzing how we ended up in a financial predicament, we try to cover our faulty financial steps with credit cards, lines of credit and overdraft protection. The next phase is more debt, more financial frustration, and less peace of mind. Handling financial crises by incurring more debt is never the answer. Debt is never, ever empowering. Debt can be managed, but will require wise choices in your finances that will educate and encourage you to make permanent changes in your spending habits that positively affect your purchasing power. Consider these wise choices to plan your own escape from debt:

- **Plan how you will spend your money.** Develop a plan for your money. Develop financial goals and review them constantly. Keep your goals always before you and focus on what you want to accomplish financially. Plan how you are going to spend, save, and invest your income.

- **Track where your money is going.** Keep track of where you spend your money for the next 30 days. This will assist in determining where you can cut costs and will assist in determining the true costs for developing a spending plan. Review and balance your checkbook monthly. Track your cash inflow and outflow.

- **Stop using your credit card.** If you cannot pay cash, then choose not to make the purchase. If you must use your credit card, then pay the balance in full before the statement arrives. Stop using your credit cards and make use of a debit card that deducts money directly from your checking account.

- **Work on reducing or eliminating the number of creditors you owe.** Debt-free is the goal. Develop a plan to pay off all outstanding debts. Start with the smallest creditor and continue to pay that debt until paid in full. Continue this process until you are completely free from creditors.

- **Call creditors and develop a plan to repay debts.** Set up a plan with your creditors to repay all debts. Keep your word since your payment of debts will and can affect your credit report.

- **Decide NOT to accumulate any additional debts.** It takes a dedicated, disciplined individual who will decide NOT to incur any additional debts.

- **Minimize ATM usage.** Each trip to the ATM machine costs you time and money. Every $1.50 to $3.00 for each ATM transaction is a waste of your hard-earned dollars.

- **Look for opportunities to save money.** Take your lunch to work at least 2 days a week. Discontinue or reduce your cable services. Stop subscriptions to magazines that you subscribe to and do not read. Identify areas in your financial world where you are wasting money and take proactive steps to make corrective actions.

- **Eat out less** and **entertain at home.** Stop for a period of time until you reduce your debt to a manageable level.

Eating out and spending money on entertainment are two areas where you can cut costs.

Decide to be debt free NOW. Debt robs you of your peace. It grows while you are sleeping. It takes away your options. It causes anxiety and stress. Debt destroys your health. Debt is not your friend. Decide now that you will be debt-free. Deciding to be debt-free is probably one of the best financial exercises that you can engage in to prolong your life. Try it. You will be amazed at how much happier you are when you are debt-free. Take an inventory of all of your creditors. The goal is to reduce or eliminate debt, so make the wise choice of not incurring additional debt, at least not any significant amount.

What You Can Do Now

- The first order of debt reduction or elimination is to pay creditors in full and promise yourself that you will make you the number one creditor in your life.

- Make it your goal to increase your net worth on a daily basis. Take the money that you would pay creditors and invest in your own financial future.

- If you want to free yourself from the bondage of debt, you must change your financial lifestyle. Identify those expenses and debts that are unnecessary. Take this example. Having a mortgage is necessary, but what about the four magazines that you subscribe to but never read? Is a $60 monthly cable bill necessary when you are heavily in debt?

Choose freedom today by living beneath your means!

It has been said that the quickest route to being wealthy is to live **beneath** your means. Yes, living on less than you earn is sure to bring peace of mind and wealth. It may be difficult initially since you may have stressfully lived above your means with the use of credit cards or credit lines. Map out a powerful financial future by living on less than you earn.

These are wise choices that will assist you in living beneath your means:

Pay cash. There is nothing quite as powerful as leaving a store owning a product and not being attached to a payment plan. Be wise and know that if you are making payments on a monthly basis, the product or item is not yours. It actually belongs to the bank or the mortgage company.

Minimize credit card use and work diligently to pay the bill in full each month before the statement arrives, thus avoiding finance charges.

Pay off debts. Focus on reducing or minimizing your debt-level. The borrower is servant to the lender. There is much power and peace in being debt-free.

Minimize impulse buying. Determine what triggers your spending sprees. If visiting the mall entices you to spend money that you may not have, then stay home or window shop by leaving your credit card and cash at home.

Honor God with all that you earn. Acknowledge where your help comes from and always pray about your finances. Honor God in how you spend your money. When was the last time you prayed if you should make a purchase or asked if a purchase was a wise use of your money? You can avoid many financial blunders by praying about the matter prior to making a purchase.

Pay yourself. Get into the habit of systematically paying yourself as if you are a creditor. Be indebted to your financial future by depositing into your own life.

Be grateful. I am a firm believer that when you are grateful, you open your heart to receiving more.

Credit Card Management

Would you go to a bank and borrow money to buy a pair of shoes? How about applying for a loan to purchase an outfit that you must have? Most people would answer no, yet this is essentially what you are doing when you use your credit card to purchase frivolous 'I must have' items. Having many credit cards may have been fashionable at one time, but today, being in debt is not fashionable or healthy. Paying cash still reigns supreme. Unfortunately, the life of the average American is riddled with debt, and most of it results from credit card use. I find it interesting that the words **debt** and **death** sound so much alike. Being in debt can kill and steal your joy. Do not allow improper use of credit cards to be a burden to you.

Here are a few basic steps to wise management of your credit card:
- Keep your receipts of purchases made during the month and verify the purchases on your credit card statement monthly.

- Decide that if you cannot pay the bill in full when the statement arrives, then do not purchase the item on your credit card.

- Resolve to use your credit card ONLY for rental car and airline reservations. However, pay cash when settling the bill.

- Pay more than the minimum balance each month.

- If possible, pay the credit card balance in full each month.

- Pay the bill BEFORE the payment due day to avoid late payments and interest.

- If you are over your credit card limit, attempt to pay at least the amount over the credit card limit immediately to avoid paying an 'over the limit' fee, which can be as high as $25.00 a month.

- Instead of using a credit card, use a check card. With a check card, funds are automatically withdrawn from your checking account when the purchase is made, thus no bill at the end of the month.

- When you get a new credit card, read the fine print. In many instances, companies offer low interest rates initially to get your business, and that rate is only available for a limited time.

Credit Repair

There is a large possibility that not managing your money properly has negatively affected your credit rating. A good credit rating is a powerful and important part of your financial wellness. Many do not realize just how important a good credit rating is until they are denied credit for loans to purchase homes, cars, or other items. For a variety of reasons, numerous individuals find themselves in a position with "not so great" or even "bad" credit ratings. Perhaps your credit problems began in college when you "over did it" with those easy to get credit cards and then could not afford to pay the bills when they arrived. For others, unforeseen circumstances such as a lost job, a financial setback due to a death in their family, or unexpected health bills may have left them with creditors and bills that they could not pay. Whatever the reason, the time is now to improve your credit rating so that you can be in a position to prosper financially in the future!

Here are 8 steps that you can take to start rebuilding your credit:

1. **Understand your current income and expenses**. To focus on any financial goal, you must assess your current situation. Before fixing the past, make sure that you are effectively taking care of the present. Develop a system to determine how much income is received and how many expenses are incurred each month. This is known as a budget, and for some people this conjures such negative images. Whatever you call it - budget, financial plan, spending plan – you need to develop one to list and track your expenses against your present income.

2. **Check your credit report.** You can write or call to request a copy of your credit report from all three of the 'big' credit bureaus: Equifax (800-685-1111); Experian (888-397-3742); and TransUnion (800-916-8800). There is usually a fee, between $7 to $10 (unless you have been denied credit, then a copy of your credit report is free). Unfortunately, erroneous information does appear occasionally in credit files, and it is up to you to take the initiative to correct the errors. Speak with a representative at the credit bureau to assist you in understanding the credit report. If you disagree with any of the information, dispute it, either in writing to the credit bureau or by calling. The credit bureau will send the information to the creditor to verify your information in an effort to settle the dispute. The creditor has 30 days to respond. The credit bureau must remove any information that is not correct on your report, but you must take the initiative to surface the issue. Make sure to get a copy of your credit report from the three bureaus since different creditors report to different bureaus.

3. **Pay off past due accounts.** Armed with a goal to rebuild your credit, you can take one of the best steps - pay off past due accounts. Even if the debt is 60 to 90 days past due, a paid off debt is a step in the right direction to rebuild your credit! It also puts integrity in the situation - acknowledging that the debt belongs to you and you

are taking the responsible route by repaying those who trusted you with their goods, services and money. This goes a long way in the rebuilding process.

4. **Contact your creditors**. If you are current and up-to-date on your financial obligations for a period of time, request that your creditors update the information on your credit report. If you are past due in paying your creditors, tell them of your intent to pay, including how much and when. Be sure to keep your word since this is also a step in the right direction to rebuilding your credit.

5. **Include a statement in your credit report**. To explain extenuating circumstances that result in damaged credit ratings, you can include a statement on your credit report so that when a creditor reviews your report, there is a valid reason for the late payments and past due bills. Maybe you had unexpected surgery and became unemployed for an extended period of time. Valid reasons for the negative information in your report could make a difference in a creditor granting or denying you credit.

6. **Create a 'peace of mind' account**. This is also known as an emergency fund. 'Peace of mind' money is an excellent way to provide a cushion for unplanned financial responsibilities. Save until you have enough money to cover your monthly expenses for at least 2 to 4 months. If that seems impossible as you pay off debts,

save a portion of all income until you reach a comfortable financial cushion. Any amount saved is a step in the right direction!

7. **Consider seeking advice from a credit counseling service.** A large amount of debt can be overwhelming, and to get a better perspective, you may want an outsider to guide you. The process of rebuilding your credit can be a daunting one, but it is possible. A credit counseling service can also provide assistance to create a budget and determine a plan to repay your debts. Do your homework before selecting a credit counseling service. Beware of services that guarantee to "clean up" your bad credit rating for a sum of money. This rarely or never happens. Keep in mind that a trip to a credit counseling service does show on your credit report and may be perceived negatively.

8. **Check your credit report annually**. An annual credit report checkup can help to avoid any unexpected errors on your credit file. I recommend requesting a copy of your credit report annually. Keep focused on rebuilding your credit. It can be done and yes, you can do it! Make it your business from this point forward to maintain a healthy credit rating.

DEBT MANAGEMENT

"It is easy to be rich and not haughty; it is difficult to be poor and not grumble."
                                        Confucius

CHAPTER 8

Education and Excellence

If you are to become a wealthy woman, you have to make it your business to get educated about the essentials of money management. It is so empowering to gain the knowledge needed to make wise decisions that positively impact the day-to-day management of your finances as well as your financial future. Education about basic money management affords you the ability to make wise decisions that affect you financially, physically, as well as emotionally. Getting better at managing your finances requires a concerted effort which includes dedicating a few hours a week reading and educating yourself. When you are informed, you always make better decisions. When you have all of the necessary information, a can-do-attitude about your finances will motivate you to make lasting positive changes in your finances. Education about money matters is so important for a woman to manage her money with pride and definitely leads to excellence in all areas of her life.

Commit to getting educated about managing your money with pride by taking the following action steps:

- Decide to spend 30 minutes a week reading a magazine, book or article on finances or a subject related to financial matters. Education is the key to moving toward wealthy living.
- Make it your goal to attend at least one finance seminar annually.
- Attend a tax course so that you are at least aware of the basics of tax preparation and tax laws that govern personal income taxes.
- Listen to tapes that educate, motivate and inspire you to get your finances in order.
- Seek financial advice.
- Join a women's group whose goal is to empower women financially.
- Teach your children what you currently know about money management. Your son's or daughter's questions will prompt you to search for answers and get more educated about money matters.

- Take an investment course at your local community college.
- If you have a financial planner or tax advisor, spend time asking questions about what you do not understand regarding money matters. Educating you as she/he manages and advises you about your money matters should be included in the fee that you pay.

It is your financial life, so the more informed you are, the better your decisions. It is fine to have someone manage your finances for you because you do not have the time to do so. However, it is essential that you obtain the knowledge and understand the decisions made that will affect your financial future. Financial education leads to excellence in all areas of your life.

Excellence

You can achieve whatever financial independence that you decide you want. It will take, however, an attitude of excellence in every area of your life. Financial management impacts you and touches all areas of your life. You can excel in the area of money management, but it takes commitment. I believe that as we get educated and motivated about organizing our finances, we move toward excellence. It is amazing to me the power, energy and smarts that women possess. They can manage households and corporations. They own television and radio stations. They birth, nurture and educate their children. They obtain college educations and become college presidents. Yet, many women allow their own financial future to languish unattended and unplanned. The paradigm is shifting for women as it relates to money. They are becoming more aware and are taking strides toward financial freedom. You must continue the progress and focus on managing debt that debilitates you. You must save and invest regularly. You need to contribute the maximum amount that you can to your retirement. Whatever financial journey you take, go at it with energy and move toward excellence.

To excel in your finances, you must continue to get educated about money matters, take the wise choices that make a positive difference in your life and press toward your goals. Albert Einstein said, "In the middle of difficulty lies opportunity." In the midst of whatever financial difficulty or prosperous moment you are experiencing, there lies an opportunity to accomplish more and manage your finances better. Can you excel in your finances? I really do believe that you can.

"The unhappiest people are poor people with plenty of money."
                               Willie Ben Grate

CHAPTER 9

Psychology of Wealth

What hinders you from living a wealthy life? Have you ever wondered why some people live from paycheck to paycheck while others flourish financially? I believe that the way we think about money determines the amount of wealth that we accumulate. I agree that wealth encompasses abundance in all areas of our life, but the accumulation of financial means makes a difference. It seems that one woman with substantial financial means can lose all of her riches and can yet regain her financial status. She obtained financial independence once and feels mentally that she can do it again. And yes, she does it. Another woman with meager savings seems to struggle, lose the little that she has and become completely stymied in her finances forever. I believe that the difference is what you feed yourself mentally on a daily basis about your money matters. You are the sum total of your thoughts. Every financial reality that you are living is a result of your thoughts of money and financial wellness. Change your inner (mental) thinking about your finances and watch your physical surroundings change. I challenge you to positively change your words and change your life. You can scream, "Broke, busted, and disgusted," and allow those situations to be revealed in your life. Better yet, you can believe in your financial freedom and speak words that bring abundance, prosperity and peace of mind. The choice is yours. Your subconscious mind cannot take a joke, so whatever words you speak, your subconscious brings about those situations that you verbalize.

No one ever acquired any positive situation in life by hoping for the worst and expecting the least. How you think about money and your expectations of it will manifest just as you believe mentally. Yes, what you focus on in your life magnifies. I encourage you to be optimistic about your finances and always speak positively about your financial concerns. You must always look for the good in your finances, even if you are in debt. Always be diligent about speaking of abundant living and prosperity. Whether you realize it or not, what you think about money greatly affects your financial well being. You have heard the mantra over and over again: **You become what you think about**. I challenge you to think abundance. Think wealth. Think prosperity. As you create your world in the area of money matters, dream big. I believe that you can live the life you really want. I also believe that you can afford the life that you really want. It will take discipline. It may take a shift mentally in how you view your finances. Make the choices in your money matters that will give you the financial freedom that you deserve.

The financial rules of wealth creation are simple, and they can and will work for anyone, regardless of her status in life. You can be a believer in God or an atheist, but the fact still remains that if you spend less than you earn, you are beginning the first step toward financial empowerment and the road to wealthy living. You can be African-American or Caucasian, but in any culture, debt is still bondage, and the borrower is servant to the lender. You can be young or old, but the fact still remains that you must make wise choices today to affect your financial status tomorrow. Most people earn more than a million dollars in a lifetime, yet when they need the money, unwise choices have left them paralyzed in their finances. You do not have to live your life moving from one financial crisis to another. You can mentally decide what actions you will take to move to a place in your finances that empowers and assists you in living a full, prosperous life. It is a choice, and the decision begins in your mind. You have to decide.

We underestimate the power of the mind. Moving from frustration to freedom requires new thinking and a shift in your mental thoughts. Moving from enslavement to empowerment in your money matters can be achieved, but it requires 'right' thinking, positive actions, and wise choices. If you are not enjoying where you are financially, then you have to do what you have never done to get a different result in your money matters. Your mental disposition regarding your finances is a key factor. You have to mentally decide that you want to take action and be proactive about making a difference in your finances. Ponder these questions. "What am I doing financially that does not make sense?" "What stops me from obtaining the financial freedom and security that I deserve?" It is not just poor people who are in debt or who struggle financially. Individuals of great means struggle financially also. Half of the financial frustration battle is thinking optimistically and positively about your finances. What you think about money is what shows up in your life. If you think that you are poor, regardless of the amount of money that you may earn, you will become poor. You think it and so it is.

Have you ever noticed that people tend to speak such negative statements about their money and personal worth? "I am a day late and a dollar short." "I am saving for a rainy day." I really do believe that when you speak negatively about your finances, you attract those negative money situations into your life. Even if those negative situations are true, do not utter the words. Words are powerful, so choose to speak words that empower you. You need to encourage yourself in your financial matters so that you can move to a more abundant place. I believe that you should focus on those situations that bring you joy, peace and comfort in your money matters. Choose to believe that you are prospering every day. Choose to think on words and statements that empower and encourage you. For your own peace of mind and sanity, do whatever it takes mentally to move to a wealthy place. You have the resources, and you are capable of making all of the right choices to empower you financially. Live life on your own financial terms, and do what you know needs to be done in your finances. Begin to shift mentally, and you will shift financially to a more positive fiscal posture.

"Lazy hands make a woman poor, but diligent hands bring wealth."

Proverbs 10:4 (NIV)

CHAPTER 10

Choose to be Wise

Your financial stability depends on your choices regarding your money matters. Money does not cure all ills, but it does open the mind to creative solutions! Choose to be wealthy and wise, and have a total wealth package for your life. Focus on great health. Focus on those things that bring peace and serenity to your life. Focus on good loving and rid your life of toxic relationships. You must also focus on managing your money with ease and put systems in place that empower and assist you in meeting your financial goals. Whether you admit it or not, your money matters really do matter. Ignoring money matters can cause stress, insomnia, irritability and other sickness that will affect your peace of mind, your health, and your sense of security.

Now that you have started this wonderful journey as a wealthy woman, it important to decide **NOW** what steps you will take to reach your financial goals. What you decide to do now, in the early stages of accumulating wealth, will determine whether you will experience financial frustration or freedom in your money matters. Set financial goals for wealth building. Have a plan for your income. Money with no vision is pure madness! Take positive action steps today that will reap great benefits tomorrow. It is your divine right to be prosperous, so take the time to manage your wealth by beginning a journey of financial self caring and nurturing. Balance your checkbook. Bank online. Eliminate debt in your life. The choice is yours, so become the wealthy woman you can become by making wise choices.

There are many impediments to wealth building, and procrastination leads the list. To become a wealthy woman who manages her money with pride, you will need to get in motion to avoid procrastination. Put mechanisms in place that will assist you in managing your money, such as on-line banking and automatic investment from your checking account. If you hate to balance your checkbook, use a check card for your purchases. You may not keep track of the money that you spend, but the purchases will be listed on your bank statement as a reminder of what you spent. Hire a personal coach who assists you in staying the course financially. Establish a 'peace of mind' fund. You will need a financial cushion for those challenges that will surely come. If you know that financial challenges will come, why not take the necessary steps to prepare for them? Saving and investing money are essential, and you owe it to your financial future. The goal is to begin the process now. Before a layoff, divorce, or a corporate 'rightsizing' threatens your finances, take the necessary steps to establish a nest egg that will meet the challenges that you may encounter.

You have to make the wise choice of becoming the top financial planner and producer in your own life. Become a major player in your money matters. Take the initiative. Be proactive. Think and speak positively. Here are some basic wise choices that will provide a solid foundation as you begin your financial journey:

- **Plan and prepare for your financial life.** You can allow your money to manage you or you can take control and manage your money. Financial success is a deliberate process for which you plan and prepare.

- **Always pay yourself first and make YOU a priority in your finances.** Save a portion of every dollar that you earn. Treat yourself as if you are the number one liability in your life and main creditor in your personal financial world.

- **Become disciplined about spending, saving, and investing.** It is what you save and invest that will make you wealthy, not what you earn. There is a distinct difference between net worth and income.

- **Always spend less than you earn.** Do this for the rest of your life, and you will experience financial security.

- **Minimize debt.** If you must use your credit card, pay the balance in full each month before the due date, thus avoiding late fees.

- **Pay your debts and pay them on time**. Make the most of your wealth by paying your bills on time and avoid late fees and interest payments.
- **Always speaks words of prosperity**. Powerful words bring powerful results into your life.
- **Determine where your money is going** so that you can eliminate waste in your finances.

All that you do with and about your finances is a choice. Choose to be wealthy, healthy, and wise in all of your financial endeavors. Choose those actions steps that will promote wealthy living, prosperity and abundance. Choose financial steps in your money matters that bring peace of mind and unspeakable joy, and minimize the level of stress in your life to promote great health and healing. Choose wise steps that increase your net worth annually, minimize your debt level, and educate and enlighten you to take action to secure your financial future. Choose to be wealthy in your thinking by always speaking words that empower and add strength to your vision. State affirmations daily and always think positively about your finances, regardless of the orderly or disorderly state of your affairs. Choose to be wise by establishing credibility in your finances by paying your bills on time. Choose to always pay yourself first and invest for your future. Choose to be grateful by always having an attitude of gratitude. I am often amazed at the blessings and joy that appear in my life when I am grateful.

CHOOSE TO BE WISE

"If you are wise, your wisdom will reward you."

Proverbs 9:12 (NIV)

CHAPTER 11

The Conclusion of the Matter

I hope that you have been empowered to live your best financial life as you read this book. It was my intent to inspire, encourage and educate you. I also wanted to give you a motive for your actions - to make wise choices that promote pride in your money management. So many women are struggling financially, and their fiscal posture affects all areas of their lives. A single mother struggling to meet the financial needs of her children. A divorced woman entering the work force for the first time. A married woman balancing her time to manage the family finances. A widowed woman unaware of her financial status in life. These are real issues for many women, and change requires education, commitment, and action. Additionally, many women know, yet refuse to take action. You must step off the sidelines and into your own financial life and stop allowing your finances to manage you. With a little effort, you can experience more joy and financial abundance.

The conclusion of the matter is you cannot listen to your financial fears. You must confront them. A woman who listens to her fears is immobilized by inactivity. You cannot afford to be immobilized by fear and frustration about your money matters. Take action now. Never put off for tomorrow what you can do today to positively affect your financial stability. Your financial well-being is greatly affected by how much control you feel you have over your finances. You are also affected by the thoughts that you have.

I wanted to provide a myriad of wise choices for women of all ages, races, situations, and financial needs that would instill pride in managing their finances, as well as empower them toward excellence in their finances. I hear so often from women, "I need help in my finances!" It is my hope that reading this book and following the steps included will bring clarity and understanding when managing your money matters.

The conclusion of the matter is that money will either help or hinder you. It all depends on your wise management of it. Be clear about this point: it is not your income that determines your fiscal status in life. Your fiscal status in life is determined by how much you save and invest on a regular basis. You must recognize that there is a major difference between net worth and income. Recognizing this truth will affect your attitude and determine how you spend your money.

Women cannot squander their resources as a result of making unwise money management decisions. They cannot remain inactive in managing their personal finances or continue to invest too conservatively. These actions leave women with insufficient funds for their financial future. Women need to systematically and religiously invest. Focus on increasing your net income. Manage your financial anxieties. Women are faced with recessions and depression concerning financial matters. Women experience procrastination and stagnation instead of activity to secure the financial future that they want to make a reality. Women dance with debt and doubt on a daily basis because wise choices are not chosen. The conclusion of the matter is that women cannot afford to be mediocre in their actions toward building wealth. Mediocrity in financial matters is a sure failure for an unstable financial future. Financial stability is about choices.

Women are capable of enduring the most stressful of situations in life and still survive. It is my hope that all women will stop surviving and start living the full abundant life that is theirs. It is my desire that they will start being the powerful individuals that they are and stop buying and charging purchases that they feel will give them power. Money that you have is only as powerful as your wise management and use of it. The conclusion of the matter is that a wealthy woman does the following to gain financial independence and stability:

- **Lives beneath her financial means**.
- **Plans and prepares for her financial future.**
- **Invests regularly.**
- **Plans for retirement.**
- **Focuses on increasing net worth.**

- **Minimizes debt level.**
- **Owns her own business.**
- **Possesses a strong spiritual foundation.**
- **Educates herself for empowerment.**
- **Minimizes the amount of taxes paid.**
- **Speaks words of prosperity.**
- **Exhibits an attitude of gratitude.**

Decide to make wise choices to plan and prepare for your financial future and propel yourself into financial freedom and add a new level of confidence to your life. I hope that you are empowered and encouraged to manage your money with P.R.I.D.E. You deserve financial stability and security.

Enjoy the journey and affirm rich blessings for your life!

NOTES

NOTES

NOTES

NOTES

NOTES

For additional copies of
Wealthy Woman-Wise Choices
call the order line at Financially Focused
(703) 503-0795
or order online at
www.FinanciallyFocused.com